Monika Utnik-Strugała studied romance studies at the University of Warsaw in Poland and is a lifestyle and design journalist. She made her debut with a children's book about Italian culture. In Italy she likes to spend her free time in her beloved country house.

Ewa Poklewska-Koziełło was born and raised in Gdansk, Poland. There she studied architecture. She enjoys painting. She illustrated dozens of books and magazines for children.

Monika Utnik-Strugała

CHRISTMAS IS COMING

Traditions from Around the World

Illustrated by
Ewa Poklewska-Koziełło

North
South

Translated from the Polish by Antonia Lloyd-Jones

Contents

A symbolic date

We celebrate Christmas on December 25, but no one knows for sure if Jesus really was born on that day.

Can you imagine the winter without Christmas? It's one of the most important and happiest Christian holidays—full of aromas, flavors, and unforgettable traditions. And yet officially we only began to celebrate it as a special holiday quite recently, about four hundred years after the birth of Jesus, and the date adopted for it is symbolic.

Originally not very much significance was attached to the birth of Jesus. The reason was simple. Nobody knew—and to this day nobody knows—exactly when he was born. None of the four Evangelists (Jesus's disciples who described his life story in the Bible) mentioned the date of their teacher's

birth, or where exactly he was born. In fact, they weren't really concerned about it. Mark and John didn't mention it at all, while Matthew and Luke only gave a rough outline, saying that it happened in the reign of the Roman emperor Augustus; that in those days Judea was ruled by King Herod; that a population census was being carried out at the time; and that when the angel declared the news to the shepherds, they were in the pastures with their sheep. For the Evangelists and the early Christians, Jesus's death was more important than his birth (because in the Christian religion death is regarded as the start of real life—eternal life). As a result, the precise date of Christ's arrival on Earth became lost somewhere in the mists of time. And yet we celebrate Christmas on December 25. Why is that?

Depending on the year, December 21 or 22 is the time of the winter solstice, the point at which the days start to grow longer. Many ancient civilizations held wild celebrations at that time of year, joyfully acknowledging the fact that the darkness was going away at last. For example, the Romans held masquerades and jolly processions as part of a festival known as Saturnalia, in honor of Saturn, the god of agriculture; and several days later, on December 25, they had a festival in honor of the Invincible Sun. Curiously, when the authors of the Bible described Jesus, they too compared him with the sun, and Christ also called himself the "Light of the World." Christians chose December 25 as the symbolic date of Christ's birth and replaced the Roman festival with a Christian one, because just as the spring sun conquers the winter darkness, so Jesus brought humankind the hope of a better tomorrow.

The countdown begins

The best thing for helping you to endure the wait until Christmas is an Advent calendar! Traditionally, an Advent calendar was a large, flat cardboard box with twenty-four little windows. Behind each window was a delicious chocolate. Today, many Advent calendars feature cardboard "flaps" with beautiful art hidden under each flap. But have you ever wondered what the word *advent* means?

The word *advent* comes from the Latin *adventus*, which means "an arrival, a coming." It's the time of joyful anticipation of the birth of Jesus. It starts on the fourth Sunday before Christmas and continues until Christmas Eve. During this time, people make preparations for one of the most important events in the Christian religion. On the weekdays, church services known as Rorate Masses are held in honor of the Virgin Mary. Their name comes from the Latin *rorate*, which is the opening word of one of the hymns sung during the service ("*Rorate caeli desuper,*" which means "Drop down dew, O heavens, from above"). During the liturgy there's a special candle burning by the altar, known as a Rorate Candle. Rorate Masses start before dawn, when the darkness in the church is only dispelled by lighted candles or lanterns that the congregation has brought from home. Only once the church is filled with the sound of the celebratory hymn "*Gloria in excelsis Deo*" ("Glory to God in the highest") is the electric lighting switched on.

During Advent, the priests light an extra candle in the churches. The lighting of the fourth candle is a sign that Christmas has arrived. In some countries, including Germany, Hungary, Sweden, and the United States, people burn Advent candles at home as well. They stand in a wreath on the table or in a candlestick on the windowsill. The first Advent wreath was made about 180 years ago by Pastor Johann Hinrich Wichern, who ran an orphanage in Hamburg. He felt sorry for the children spending Christmas without their parents and wanted to give them a very special gift. So he attached twenty-four candles to an old wooden cartwheel, and each day one of the children lit one of the candles. Over time the number of candles was reduced to four.

Instead of buying a ready-made Advent calendar at the store, you can create one yourself: make a garland out of small cloth bags and hide a piece of candy or another small gift inside each one. You could also pin little paper bags containing chocolates to a corkboard. But don't be tempted to eat the candy on the sly!

The giant from Sweden

In the first week of Advent, an unusual straw sculpture appears in the main square of the Swedish town of Gävle. It's 23 feet high and 43 feet long, and it's in the form of a . . . goat.

The first of these giants stood in the town's marketplace in 1966. Apparently, a local businessman named Stig Gavlén came up with the idea for this original kind of decoration. But why did he put up a goat rather than a Christmas tree or a figure of Santa Claus?

It's all because, for centuries, the goat has played an important role in the lives of the people of Sweden. The Vikings, who were the ancestors of the Swedes, Norwegians, and Danes, believed that it was the favorite animal of Thor, the god of thunderstorms and lightning. His chariot was pulled by magical goats named Teeth-Barer and Teeth-Grinder. During the winter solstice the Vikings sacrificed a goat to Thor and prayed to him for an auspicious new year and a plentiful harvest. The Swedes retained an affection for the horned animal. In the festive season they decorate their homes with miniature goats, known in Swedish as *julbock*. Trimmed with red ribbons, the figurines stand on their windowsills or bureaus. The Gävle goat is their younger brother, but how big he has grown!

A hundred years ago it was customary in Sweden for the adults to dress up as julbock goats and frighten the children. The man chosen to be the goat would cover himself in animal skins, put on a goat mask with horns, and walk around the neighborhood, tricking people into giving him presents. He'd promise to leave them in peace if they gave him a nice gift in exchange. Over time the julbock didn't just stop being malicious, but changed completely—he started handing out presents to the children instead. Later he was replaced by Santa Claus, and on the Swedish Christmas cards it's a goat that pulls his sleigh.

On Saint Nicholas's Day

In some countries people celebrate their "name day"—the festival of the saint whose name they share. But on December 6, Saint Nicholas's Day, it's not just boys called Nicholas who receive gifts. Other children are given small presents on that day too.

About seventeen hundred years ago, in the town of Myra (which is in present-day Turkey) there lived a kind and very devout boy. His name was Nicholas. When his parents died, he inherited a large fortune, but instead of squandering it on fun and games, he gave away all his money to the poor. He used to leave gifts for them anonymously so they didn't know who had donated them. Even when he became a bishop he lived modestly and helped those in need. He particularly enjoyed giving presents to children because he liked making them happy. When he died, he was declared a saint. People were so impressed by his good deeds that in his memory they decided to do the same thing at least once a year. And so a new custom was born of exchanging gifts, on Saint Nicholas's Day.

Saint Nicholas leaves his presents quietly in the night of December 5 to 6. He usually puts them under your pillow, or in your shoes if you've left them beside your bed. In Germany he checks to make sure the shoes are clean, because if they're not, instead of gifts he leaves a rotten potato or a lump of coal.

Curiously, in some countries Saint Nicholas himself is given presents on his feast day. In Germany the children leave a plate of small snacks for him or put carrots in their shoes. In Belgium extra potatoes are sown in the garden plots outside people's houses for Saint Nicholas's horse to feed on. After all, that horse works very hard and deserves something in exchange too!

The luckiest children of all are the Dutch ones. Saint Nicholas appears in the Netherlands around November 11 so that he'll have time to visit every Dutch town before his feast day. But listen to this: instead of a sleigh, he arrives on a steamboat! Each year he docks at a different port, and the children greet him with a song called "Here Comes the Steamboat." Why does he come by this unusual form of transport? It's because the Netherlands is a land of sailors. In olden times the Dutch merchants' ships used to sail into the ports in November to overwinter. Looking forward to seeing their families again after a long time apart, the sailors would bring their parents gifts of various kinds. Maybe that's why a ship seems a more natural form of transport for Saint Nicholas here than a sleigh.

You'll probably also be surprised to know that the Dutch saint doesn't come from the icy wastes of the Arctic Circle but from . . . Spain. Why is that? In the past the Netherlands and Spain actively traded goods—the Dutch ships brought home beautiful objects, exotic fruits, and rare spices from the southern country. Everything that was special and unusual was associated with Spain. What's more, the bones of Saint Nicholas of Myra were preserved in the Italian city of Bari (where they remain to this day), and for some time Bari was under Spanish rule. So no wonder the Dutch say that Sinterklaas (as they call Saint Nicholas/Santa Claus) comes from the south of Europe.

Nor will you be amazed to learn that Sinterklaas travels to all the Dutch towns and cities in turn on a white horse. In the distant past people believed that the god Odin rode around on a white horse, rewarding farmers for their good work. In time Odin's role was taken over by Saint Nicholas, but the white horse remained part of the legend.

The Dutch Saint Nicholas/Santa Claus is very sympathetic, and he rewards all the children with traditional gingerbread cookies called *pepernoten*. But for their larger presents the youngest children have to wait until December 5, when the gift-giving evening (known in Dutch as *pakjesavond*) occurs. That's when Sinterklaas leaves presents on the doorstep or puts them in the shoes the children have left beside the fireplace. Sometimes, instead of a card with the recipient's name on it, he adds a funny poem that explains who the present is for.

Not every country celebrates Saint Nicholas's Day. For instance, it isn't celebrated in Sweden, Norway, Spain, Iceland, the United Kingdom, or the United States.

Grittibaenz—the man who gets baked

The Grittibaenz is a relative of the gingerbread man. His prime time in Switzerland is during the days before Christmas, when you will find him ready and waiting in most bakeries.

The little man is made with raisins for eyes and for the buttons of his jacket. Sometimes granulated sugar is used as a decoration.

How did Grittibaenz get his name? *Gritte* means "to stand with your legs apart." *Baenz* is a pet name for Benedict. But as this name was so common in the Middle Ages, it could stand for any man. And so Grittibaenz means a man standing with legs astride, which is exactly what the pastry itself looks like.

Even back in the Middle Ages people liked eating the little man—but only on special occasions. In northern France the custom arose that a child bishop should be chosen for Saint Nicholas Day (December 6). Just for the one day the normal order was reversed, and it was the child bishop who took command. The boy, all dressed up, would go through the town in a procession with the other children. But the crucial point was that he could tell the teachers off and punish all the grown-ups. During these processions, he always had the support of a Grittibaenz.

Of course you can bake your own Grittibaenz, and there are no restrictions on your imagination. You can knead the dough into all kinds of shapes with whatever decorations you like. You can dress him in unusual clothes, for example. Or maybe you'd prefer to bake a gingerbread lady?

Dancing in church

On December 8 an important Catholic feast is celebrated all over the world: the Immaculate Conception of the Blessed Virgin Mary. In Spain an unusual event takes place on that day.

It's hard to explain the exact meaning of the Immaculate Conception in just a few words. In the Christian religion there's a belief that all people are born with the burden of original sin (meaning the sin committed by Adam and Eve when they ate the forbidden fruit) and that the Virgin Mary was the only person to have avoided it. That's not easy to understand, is it? For the time being it'll be easier for you to associate this feast with another unusual event called the Dance of the Sixes (in Spanish, Baile de Los Seises), which for more than four hundred years has taken place on this day in the Spanish city of Seville.

There are two reasons why it's a remarkable dance. First, because it's performed in the cathedral, in front of the high altar—have you ever see anyone dancing in a Catholic church during mass? Second, it's not as jolly and lively as many dances are, but slow and stately, more like walking than dancing.

The dance is performed three times a year: on the feast of Corpus Christi, during Advent, and at the end of the carnival (just before the start of Lent). Every time it draws a large audience. It's divided into three parts, which are dedicated in turn to the Virgin Mary, the bishop, and the authorities and residents of Seville. It's performed by six or twelve boys dressed in brightly colored three-quarter-length pants and loose tunics based on sixteenth-century costumes. They also wear hats with feathers. The most animated part of the dance is when they beat out the rhythm on castanets (a kind of small instrument held in the hand). Yet despite its simple steps—or maybe because they are performed with such precision—the dance always makes a very strong impression.

The boys who take part in the performance often say years later that the rehearsals were tiring and difficult, but the sense of satisfaction was huge—because they were given the opportunity to dance before Jesus.

The festival of lights

On December 13 candlelit processions are held in the streets of Swedish towns and villages. This is how the Swedes pay tribute to Saint Lucy, who some seventeen hundred years ago was beheaded on this day for her faith in Jesus. The saint's name comes from the Latin word *lux*, meaning "light."

Saint Lucy lived in the days of the Roman Empire. She helped persecuted Christians who were hiding in the catacombs—underground graveyards—by bringing them food. She found her way through the dark passages by the light of candles attached to a garland that she wore on her head. Nowadays the girls who walk at the front of the candlelight processions wear similar crownlike garlands on their heads. Apparently, every little girl in Sweden dreams of playing the role of Saint Lucy at least once in her life. There are even competitions for the role, a bit like beauty contests. The little girl wearing the crown is followed by boys and girls dressed in white. They all sing religious songs and hold candles, the light of which is meant to dispel the winter darkness and also to herald the approach of the long days of summer. After the procession the Swedes go home for a celebratory dinner. The high point of it is when soft butter-and-saffron buns are served. They're called *lussekatter*, which means "saffron kitties," but people also call them Saint Lucy's eyes.

Three days earlier, on December 10, at Stockholm town hall, the Nobel Prize ceremony is held. The people who are due to receive this exceptional distinction are awoken at dawn by girls dressed in white, with flaming crowns on their heads. Apparently one of the prize winners, the American writer John Steinbeck, thought they were angels and exclaimed, "Oh God, I've died and gone to heaven!" Another laureate (whose name the organizers refuse to divulge) raced into the corridor in terror, seized a fire extinguisher, and started putting out the flaming crowns. Plainly neither of the laureates was aware of the Swedish tradition. But you wouldn't be surprised to see such a procession by now!

Sweden isn't the only country to celebrate the festival of lights. On the night from December 7 to 8, the cities of Colombia are illuminated by merry little flames as well. It's called La Noche de las Velitas: the Night of the Little Candles. The porches, yards, and windowsills are decorated with larger and smaller candles, and pyramid-shaped lanterns. In the town of Quimbaya the residents arrange the lanterns in elaborate configurations on the sidewalks, and the most interesting one wins a prize. In places located on the ocean they launch little boats with small candles attached to them. But the capital city, Bogota, shines with the brightest lights on December 7, when the night ends with a firework display.

Meanwhile, in San Fernando in the Philippines, on the last Saturday before Christmas, the darkness is dispelled by huge, brightly colored decorations that pulsate with light to the beat of music coming from loudspeakers. Since 1904, a competition has been held here as part of the Ligligan Parul (meaning the Giant Lantern Festival), in which the best decoration wins.

It all began quite simply, with candles. The Filipinos would bring them to masses known as novenas (from *novem*, the Latin word for "nine"), which are held on each of the nine days leading up to Christmas. To stop the winter wind from blowing out the flames along the way, they put the candles inside lanterns made of paper or bamboo. No one knows exactly when and why, but in time the lanterns grew to giant proportions, and nowadays they look more like huge shining rosettes. The lanterns entered for the contest are sometimes several yards in diameter and have steel rims. The candles were replaced long ago by lightbulbs—a single lantern may contain as many as ten thousand of them! Preparations for the contest take weeks, although the actual display only goes on for about a quarter of an hour. But the effort pays off because the fabulously colorful constructions are admired by all, and there's a large cash prize for the winner.

At the Christmas fair

As we all know, in days of old there weren't any shopping malls. People did their shopping at open-air markets. In Germany, Christmas fairs were especially popular, and they still are to this day. There are more than 150 of them throughout the country, sometimes several at once in the same city!

In the past these fairs attracted people from every corner of the surrounding area. Here they could buy supplies to see them through the winter and also stock up on special treats for the festive season. Sellers of luxury goods and craftsmen would set out their wares in the town's main square and the neighboring streets. They sold everything you can possibly imagine: eggs, bread, meat and vegetables, baskets, scarves, sheepskins, and beads, as well as horses, chickens, and pigs. Meanwhile, wandering minstrels and jugglers roamed among the market traders. Gypsy women told fortunes, and small theater troupes provided entertainment for the weary shoppers. These fairs didn't just allow people to do business; they also gave people an opportunity to get together before Christmas.

Christmas fairs are still organized to this day in various countries. The most famous ones include the German kind, known as the Weihnachtsmarkt. Just as in the past, you can buy the local specialties at these fairs, including cooked meats, cheese, candy, and handcrafted items: wooden toys, Christmas decorations, traditional pottery, and regional fabrics. But those are not the only attractions available. The Weihnachtsmarkt is a bit like a funfair, because as well as the stalls selling goods there are also skating rinks, carousels, and a large tower, often with a spiral slide, from the top of which you can see a panorama of the town and the twinkling lights of all the stalls below. At the center of each fair stands a Christmas tree in all its splendor (the city of Dortmund boasts the tallest one, which is almost 150 feet high, with the figure of an angel on top). Sometimes a tall pyramid (a moving construction that looks like a wedding cake with figurines) appears too, a huge music box, or an edible figure named Pflaumentoffel made of dried plums and candy.

Germany's oldest Christmas fair is held in Dresden, and it's called the Striezelmarkt, from *Striezel*, which is the name of a traditional short-crust pastry with an apple filling. Every year the local confectioners bake a giant cake of this kind, then ceremonially cut it into slices in the central marketplace and hand the treat out to passers-by.

Another famous fair is held in the city of Augsburg. It opens with a performance by twenty-four actors dressed as angels. The characters appear one by one in the windows of the town hall, playing instruments and singing.

The town hall in Meissen also puts on a spectacular display during the Advent season by transforming itself into . . . an Advent calendar. Behind twenty-four of its blue window shutters there are hidden surprises. The staff who work at the town hall reveal one of these items each day, and people can place bids for them. Would you like to try your luck in the raffle?

From sprig to tree

The ancient Romans decked the trees to appeal to the god of the harvest for good crops. On the shortest day of the year, the Egyptians adorned their houses with palm leaves to remind them of the summer. But why do we decorate our Christmas trees?

Apparently, it was a monk named Boniface who chose a conifer as the Christmas tree. One day when he was living among the Celts (the indigenous inhabitants of what is now Germany), he cut down a great oak, which for the pagan tribe was a magical tree. As it fell to the ground, the tree destroyed the plants growing around it, apart from one small fir tree. Boniface saw this as a miracle. "You see, this small fir tree is mightier than your oak," he said. "And it's an evergreen. The Lord God is just as strong and eternal." So the legend goes. But in actual fact . . .

For centuries people saw magical properties in coniferous trees, because they don't lose their color or drop their needles, not even in the hardest winter. The Slavs used to cut off a branch of pine, spruce, or fir and hang it close to the ceiling to protect them from diseases. Decked with fruits, nuts, and paper cutouts, the *podłaźniczka*, as this Slavic decoration was called, was also meant to guarantee prosperity and love. When it dried out, it was never thrown away. It was ground and added to the animal feed or buried in the fields so that the crops would be plentiful.

The Christmas trees familiar to us today first appeared about five hundred years ago in Alsace, a region on the border of Germany and France. The Alsatians decorated them with apples, which were associated with paradise; gingerbread cookies, which were to guarantee good health; and nuts, which symbolized strength. The Alsatian custom of decorating the Christmas tree very slowly spread throughout Europe, first to royal courts and among the aristocracy. In the villages the Christmas tree became fashionable comparatively recently, less than one hundred years ago. The Polish highlanders had an unusual approach to them: they would hang a small tree from the ceiling, upside down, and decorate it with candies. It was an ingenious design, because at any point you could lower the tree by pulling on a string and easily reach for a treat.

Nowadays many people buy artificial Christmas trees. Do you know who invented them? In the late-nineteenth century the Germans were far too eager to chop down conifer forests in search of the perfect Christmas tree; sometimes one family had several of them in their house. To put a stop to the mass felling, a ban on having more than one tree was introduced. Then someone came up with the idea of selling artificial Christmas trees, consisting of a wooden frame with branches attached to it, made of goose feathers dyed green. And the idea caught on. Over time it was improved on by the Americans. First they used Christmas trees made of animal hair, produced by the same method as brushes, then trees made of aluminum and then finally of plastic.

A Christmas tree doesn't have to be a tree. Popular interior design magazines will try to convince us that we can make one out of an unfolded ladder, for example. If you have a postcard collection, you can hang the cards on a corkboard in the shape of a fir tree. Or you can pin a light garland to the wall.

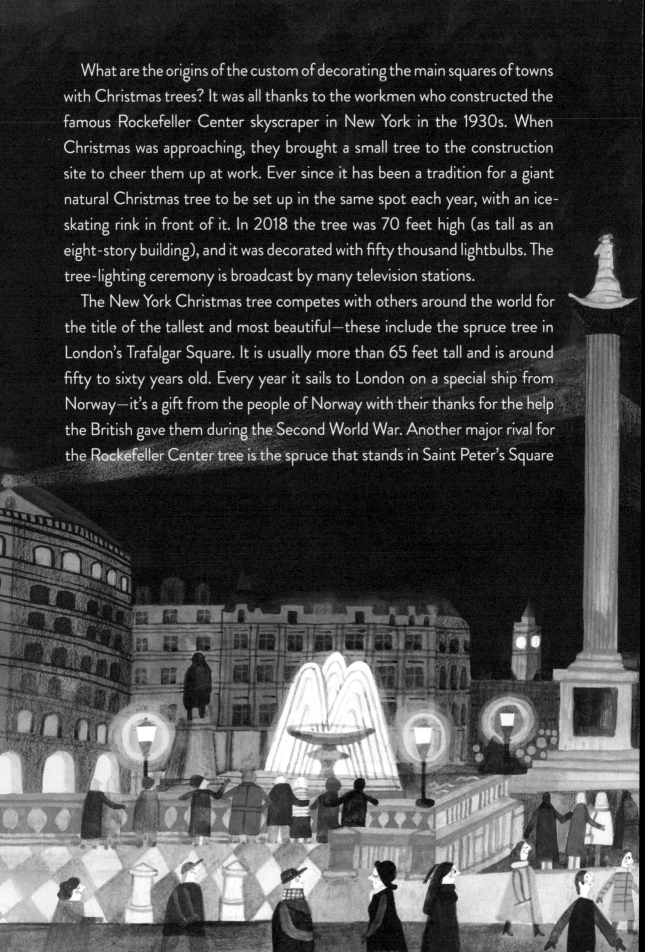

What are the origins of the custom of decorating the main squares of towns with Christmas trees? It was all thanks to the workmen who constructed the famous Rockefeller Center skyscraper in New York in the 1930s. When Christmas was approaching, they brought a small tree to the construction site to cheer them up at work. Ever since it has been a tradition for a giant natural Christmas tree to be set up in the same spot each year, with an ice-skating rink in front of it. In 2018 the tree was 70 feet high (as tall as an eight-story building), and it was decorated with fifty thousand lightbulbs. The tree-lighting ceremony is broadcast by many television stations.

The New York Christmas tree competes with others around the world for the title of the tallest and most beautiful—these include the spruce tree in London's Trafalgar Square. It is usually more than 65 feet tall and is around fifty to sixty years old. Every year it sails to London on a special ship from Norway—it's a gift from the people of Norway with their thanks for the help the British gave them during the Second World War. Another major rival for the Rockefeller Center tree is the spruce that stands in Saint Peter's Square in the Vatican (in 2018 it was 70 feet tall), which comes straight from the Alps. The custom of setting up a Christmas tree outside the cathedral was started by the Polish pope, John Paul II, in 1982.

Of course, some Christmas trees are even taller, such as the one in the German city of Dortmund, which is 150 feet high. However, they're not natural trees but are built out of smaller spruces or fir trees supported by scaffolding.

Yet not even these can rival the record holder from the town of Gubbio in Italy, which is regarded as the world's tallest Christmas tree though it is artificial. It is 2,130 feet high (the length of six soccer fields!) and 1,150 feet wide at its base. It is formed out of thousands of lanterns positioned on the slope of Mount Ingino. Rivaling it for originality is the tree in Rio de Janeiro, which is a floating tree. A steel structure carries it on the waters of Rodrigo de Freitas Lagoon. It's more than 230 feet tall, and it's lit by more than nine hundred thousand LED lightbulbs.

Glossy glass wonders

A Christmas tree decked with apples, nuts, and candies—that was a beautiful thing! You just had to reach out a hand and a treat fell into your mouth. How did those edible decorations come to be replaced by ornaments? Here's the story.

Since time immemorial the German town of Lauscha has been famous for products made of glass; windowpanes, medicine bottles, richly decorated goblets, and jewelry are all made here. But in the mid-nineteenth century the local glassworks was not doing as well as in the past, and its workers were sinking into poverty. Then along came the Christmas holiday, and the children wanted to decorate their Christmas trees with apples and walnuts, according to the custom of the times. But not many parents could afford these ornaments. And that was when, to avoid disappointing his own children, a humble glassworks employee named Hans Greiner used a red-hot glass tube to blow fruits made of glass. The joy was endless!

Hans's unique Christmas tree decorations were so admired by his neighbors that they began to make similar ones of their own. Soon the owner of the glassworks became interested in them, and production took off at high speed. You could say Hans's ornaments saved the glassworks from bankruptcy.

The ornaments only really became famous about fifteen years later. One day, at a store owned by the American businessman Frank W. Woolworth in Lancaster, Pennsylvania, a traveling salesman appeared, offering to sell some of the ornaments from Lauscha. Woolworth didn't like the decorations, so he only bought a few, and did so with great reluctance, just for the sake of peace and quiet. But when his compatriots turned out to be thrilled with them, he started to import the ornaments from Germany in large numbers—as many as two hundred thousand each year!

Before the glass ornaments appeared, Christmas trees were mainly decked with good things to eat: fruits, gingerbread cookies, marzipan, and candies wrapped in shiny silver foil. Candies, pinecones, and walnuts painted gold were hung on the tree too, alongside stars cut out of paper and eggs that were blown to make angels and birds with round bellies. Other Christmas tree toys and chains were made of straw. Curiously, Christmas decorations were also cut out of Holy Communion wafers! In the past, instead of the fairy lights we have today, there were ordinary wax candles—you had to make sure none of them tipped over and set the tree alight! Some things were bought at the market, such as angel hair, white powder for sprinkling on the branches of the tree, or cotton wool to look like snow. But most decorations were made at home— conjured up by the children. Maybe you could try your skills too?

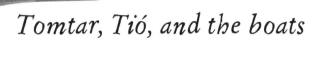

Tomtar, Tió, and the boats

The Christmas tree is definitely the most popular seasonal decoration, but it's not the only one. See what other ornaments appear in houses around the world.

In Sweden the straw julbock goat (which we met on page 14) is accompanied by gnomes dressed in gray, called tomtar. They wear hats pulled down over their eyes, with only their noses sticking out from underneath. Long ago, people believed the tomtar helped with minor household tasks, and so on holidays the housewives would leave them a bowl of groats to say thank-you. Another kind of popular Swedish decoration are illuminated paper or plastic stars, called in Swedish *julstjärna*. They refer to the Star of Bethlehem, said to have guided the three kings to the stable.

They're hung in the windows so that, like the original star, they can show travelers the way. The first of these stars appeared around 160 years ago in the German town of Herrnhut. It was made by P. H. Verbeek, a math teacher, for a geometry class so his students would understand what spatial figures looked like. In time, the twenty-five-point paper stars stopped serving as study aids and became Christmas decorations. On the first Sunday of Advent Mr. Verbeek's students decorated the school and their houses with them. Every year, Mr. Verbeek improved the design of his stars until finally he founded a manufacturing firm (which still exists to this day and is named Herrnhuter) and began to export paper decorations. That was how the stars made their way to Sweden, where the number of points was reduced to five, six, or seven.

In America the essential Christmas decorations include stockings hung above the fireplace. Santa Claus puts the presents inside them after squeezing his way down the chimney. The custom was begun by Saint Nicholas of Myra. One day he decided to help three impoverished young women by giving them some money. By chance they happened to be drying their stockings above the fire, so the gold coins fell inside them. Nowadays the children's names are usually sewn onto the American stockings so the gifts will go to the right recipient.

As well as stockings, snow globes also appear in American homes. They gained popularity in the late-nineteenth century, thanks to an Austrian named Erwin Perzy. He was working on a special lamp for surgeons to provide the ideal lighting for operating theaters. One day he dropped some tiny specks of aluminum into a bottle of water. The specks reflected the light, and they reminded him of snow, so instead of a lamp he decided to make a Christmas

decoration. Soon he founded a factory and started selling snow globes all over the world. The Americans liked them the best.

Importantly, the residents of the United States decorate their homes not just on the inside, but outside too. They're experts at illumination. They deck the trees and the fronts of buildings with Christmas lights. And as if that weren't enough, they put inflatable figures of Santa, angels, and snowmen in their front yards.

In Greece, where the sea plays a major role in the life of the local people, models of boats trimmed with lights take the lead; in private houses they're tiny, but in the city centers they're life-size. They're a reminder of the fact that after the birth of Jesus Christ the world became entirely different, like a ship taking a new course. On top of that, the Greeks hang little bells above the fireplace, which are there to warn them if naughty little goblins, called in Greek *kallikantzaroi*, appear in the house. These cross-eyed, misshapen figures never harm anyone, but they get up to all kinds of mischief: they spill the flour, bathe in the olive oil, and make the milk go sour.

In the Spanish region of Catalonia the Tió de Nadal is popular, a log that's hollowed out in the middle, with a funny face painted on it and a red cap. Through the successive days of Advent the log "sits" at the table with the family and is "fed" candy. Finally, on December 24, the children carry it under the Christmas tree, cover it with a blanket, strike it with sticks, and sing, "Little log, do a poop." Then they take off the blanket, and candies spill out of the log for the children to gobble up at once.

A miniature stable

Little houses, tiny sheep, and furniture small enough for elves. On via San Gregorio Armeno you can buy everything you need to build your own Nativity crib.

You can go shopping all year round on this famous street in the Italian city of Naples, but it's in the days before Christmas that the owners of the stores here put their most beautiful wares on display: figurines of various sizes, little wooden houses, small lanterns, and miniature stalls selling fruit, pots, and utensils. Are all their customers elves and dwarves? No way! The teeny-tiny items are used by the Italians to decorate their Christmas cribs (the Italian word for them is *presepio*), which are models made of wood and plaster, representing the birthplace of Jesus. The grotto, cave, or—as the most popular story goes—stable usually stands to one side and is just an excuse for showing everyday life in Italy. So in the foreground we can see stores, a smithy, and a mill. There's a baker taking bread out of the oven, traders on their way to market with baskets of oranges, and a smith shoeing a horse; and there are some shepherds coming down from the highland pastures with flocks of sheep as white as snow. Moss-coated plaster cliffs tower in the background, with an artificial waterfall flowing down them.

Apparently, it was Saint Francis of Assisi who invented the Christmas crib. In 1223, at a place named Greccio, he built a real stable with a large manger; and he brought in a live cow, a horse, a donkey, and some sheep (nowadays Saint Francis's crib is the inspiration for the special shows known as Nativity plays, in which children act the roles of the Holy Family and of shepherds in a natural setting).

Over time the stables grew smaller, and the live animals were replaced by wooden or plaster figurines. To begin with, the cribs decorated church altars. One of the first was located in the Basilica of Santa Maria Maggiore in Rome (relics of the manger are still kept there, meaning pieces of wood regarded as genuine fragments of Christ's crib from the original stable in Bethlehem). The crib was sculpted in marble by the famous sculptor Arnolfo di Cambio in 1291. It became a model for others and survives to this day. We can see an equally historic stable, dating back more than three hundred years, at the San Martino Museum in Naples. It's known as the Cuciniello, which was the family name of its first owner; and it includes eight hundred wooden figurines of shepherds, animals, and other items!

Christmas cribs are also popular in Spain, and the Spanish word for them is *belén*. A detail that distinguishes them from the Italian cribs is a figure known as el caganer, who features in cribs from the Catalonia region in particular. He's usually in the shape of a man, squatting to one side, with his pants down; and he's doing a . . . poop. According to tradition, this figure is meant to bring in a good harvest in the new year because his poop will fertilize the soil and make the crops more abundant. In the past, el caganer was a farmer or a shepherd. Nowadays he often has the face of a famous person: a politician, a sportsman, or a movie star. We can buy an el caganer figure that looks like former US president Donald Trump, the footballer Cristiano Ronaldo, or the singer Michael Jackson.

The Poles have their own special crib-making tradition, though it's slightly overshadowed by the Christmas tree. The cribs from the city of Kraków, known in Polish as *szopki*, are particularly famous. But curiously, these cribs don't look anything like a modest wooden stable. They're more like a castle or a church, with towers shooting into the sky and richly decorated gates inside which, above the sleeping baby Jesus, the figures of festively dressed Kraków townsfolk keep watch. The cribs are inspired by one of the city's most famous historic buildings, the Gothic Saint Mary's Basilica. The tradition of making them has been added to the UNESCO List of Intangible Cultural Heritage.

Who's going to be a millionaire?

In Spain, on December 22, it's hard to focus on your work. The country's residents are tightly gripping the lottery tickets they've bought in the hope of winning the top prize. The drawing for the lucky numbers is held during the great holiday Lotería de Navidad: the Christmas lottery.

The lottery was established in 1811, and ever since it has taken place each year just before Christmas. Not even the civil war that was fought in Spain more than eighty years ago could interrupt the lottery. The Lotería de Navidad is famous for the fact that the jackpot, called El Gordo (which means "the fat one"), is the biggest in the world. As well as that, there are seventeen other categories in which you can win cash prizes. So it's worth trying your luck!

The game is a bit like Mega Millions in the United States but slightly more complicated. The participants buy tickets with five-figure numbers printed on them. As the tickets are expensive, some people only buy one; but the same number can appear on more than one ticket, so if it's picked, all those with a ticket showing that number will share the jackpot. The lottery tickets first go on sale in the summer, but most of them are bought in December. Every day long lines form outside the famous Doña Manolita kiosk in Madrid.

When December 22 comes, the Spanish streets are deserted because everyone's watching the drawing with bated breath (the event is broadcast live on Spanish television). The lottery is preceded by a long advertisement, specially filmed for the occasion, in which famous Spanish actors and celebrities often take part.

The event lasts for around five hours! That's because a great many numbers are drawn. The wooden balls with the winning numbers on them are traditionally picked out by children from the San Ildefonso school who announce the results by . . . singing them! It's an exciting adventure for the students chosen to do this, and they spend all year preparing for it. For many years only boys were given the honor, but now the lots are drawn by girls as well. When they announce the good news to the lucky winners, they must feel a bit like Santa Claus, don't you think?

Christmas plants

Some of them are green, even though it's winter. Others are in bloom. Alongside the Christmas tree, they create a unique festive atmosphere.

☉ **Mistletoe.** On the trees it looks like a huge bird's nest. It has tiny leaves and white fruits with sticky flesh inside them. Traditionally, a few sprigs are hung in the passages between rooms. Anyone who kisses under the mistletoe will be lucky in love. Some people tell fortunes from mistletoe: if the plant preserves its color as it dries out, the year ahead will bring prosperity.

For centuries mistletoe has been regarded as a magical plant. For the Celts it was a divine gift: anyone who obtained it became as strong as the gods. While harvesting the plant during the winter solstice, they had to take care not to let it touch the ground; otherwise it lost its power. The Scandinavians in their turn believed that the little white fruits of mistletoe were the tears of the goddess Frigg, whose son was killed in an uneven fight. The goddess gave mistletoe to the human beings as a gift to warn them against hatred and war. The plant became a symbol of love and peace.

These ancient beliefs are strangely at odds with the true properties of mistletoe, because there's no hiding the fact that it's a parasite. It grows on trees, sucking nutrients from them. What's more, its fruits are poisonous for people (though waxwings and mistle thrushes can eat them without any harm). Yet it's hard to deny its charms. So let's just kiss beneath it and leave it at that!

● **Holly.** Holly has sharp, waxy leaves, but even in midwinter it remains green and succulent (that's why, along with other similar plants, it's known as an evergreen). It also boasts bloodred fruits. Truly Christmasy colors! The plant was known to the ancient Romans, who believed that its leaves could frighten off evil spirits. In days of old, the Scots also used to hang sprigs of holly on their doors to keep away mischievous elves. A holly bush was like a guard protecting the house from misfortune. Today it's most popular in Great Britain. The British plant holly in their gardens, and in December they decorate Christmas wreaths with it. The cut sprigs stay green and don't wilt at a low or a high temperature, so they're a pretty sight throughout the Christmas season.

And now here's a question for Harry Potter fans: what tree was the young wizard's magic wand made of? It was made of holly!

Poinsettia. This plant comes from Mexico, and it has lots of names. Its botanical name is *Euphorbia pulcherrima*, and in some languages it's known as "wolf-milk" or as the "Christmas star." The Aztecs, who were the ancient inhabitants of Mexico, called it the "flaming flower" and believed that it was colored by the blood of a goddess whose heart was broken by unrequited love. The plant is named "poinsettia" for Joel Roberts Poinsett, who lived two hundred years ago and was America's first ambassador to Mexico—he was the man who first brought it to the United States. But it's said to symbolize the Star of Bethlehem because its color-changing leaves (not its flowers, which are tiny and unattractive) form the typical shape of a star.

There's a legend associated with this plant. Long ago there was a poor girl who lived in Mexico. When the festive season came, she longed to give Jesus a

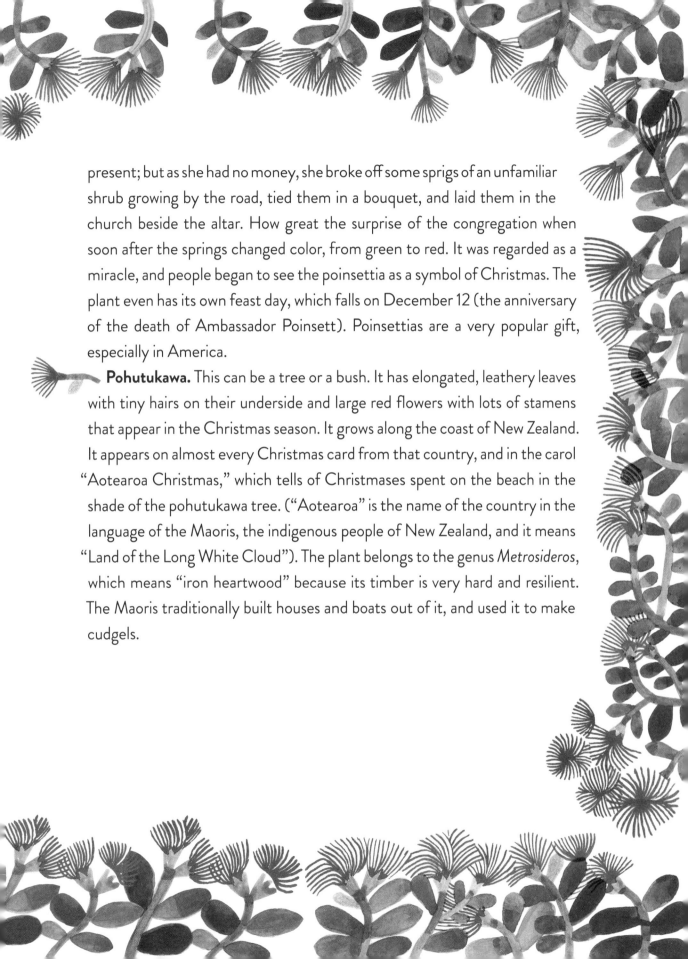

present; but as she had no money, she broke off some sprigs of an unfamiliar shrub growing by the road, tied them in a bouquet, and laid them in the church beside the altar. How great the surprise of the congregation when soon after the springs changed color, from green to red. It was regarded as a miracle, and people began to see the poinsettia as a symbol of Christmas. The plant even has its own feast day, which falls on December 12 (the anniversary of the death of Ambassador Poinsett). Poinsettias are a very popular gift, especially in America.

Pohutukawa. This can be a tree or a bush. It has elongated, leathery leaves with tiny hairs on their underside and large red flowers with lots of stamens that appear in the Christmas season. It grows along the coast of New Zealand. It appears on almost every Christmas card from that country, and in the carol "Aotearoa Christmas," which tells of Christmases spent on the beach in the shade of the pohutukawa tree. ("Aotearoa" is the name of the country in the language of the Maoris, the indigenous people of New Zealand, and it means "Land of the Long White Cloud"). The plant belongs to the genus *Metrosideros*, which means "iron heartwood" because its timber is very hard and resilient. The Maoris traditionally built houses and boats out of it, and used it to make cudgels.

May we stay the night here?

What if strangers were to knock at your door and ask to stay the night? What would you do?

The show starts at dusk. The light of a single candle illuminates a very strange procession. In the middle, a girl dressed as the Virgin Mary rides on a donkey, and there's a boy playing the role of Saint Joseph accompanying her. The couple is surrounded by children dressed as angels, little shepherd boys, musicians, and townsfolk. The procession stops at each house in turn. Joseph knocks at the door, sings, and then asks for shelter; but every time he gets a refusal. So they keep going, until at last they reach a house whose owners welcome the wandering travelers with open arms (in a small place it might be the local mayor's house, and in a larger one it could be the town hall, the cultural center, or a museum). The next day it all starts again, but this time someone else receives Mary and Joseph into his or her home.

These unusual processions parade along the streets of Mexican towns and villages for nine days, from December 16 to 24. They're known as Las Posadas. In Spanish, the word *posadas* means an inn, accommodation, or shelter. It's a reminder of the wanderings of Mary and Joseph as they sought in vain for somewhere to stay the night in Bethlehem, until finally the weary couple took refuge in a lowly stable. Each of the nine days symbolizes one month of Mary's pregnancy.

The house that eventually welcomes Mary and Joseph is chosen in advance and then beautifully decorated. The evening ends with a snack and breaking open the piñata. The piñata is a plaster or paper star hung from the ceiling (sometimes it's a ball, a vessel, or a figurine shaped like a llama) with candy hidden inside it. The challenge is to break open the piñata with a stick while blindfolded. With family and friends gathered around, in turn each of the children tries his or her best, until finally the star breaks open and showers the child in candies. The game has a deeper message too: the piñata symbolizes our battle against sin. If we trust in God (our faith is represented by the blindfold) and our loved ones (the assembled company, who call out to tell us where to strike with the stick), we will conquer our sins (we'll break open the piñata) and receive a reward (the candy).

But that's not the last of the Mexican attractions. All over the country, on December 23 the Night of the Radishes is celebrated. Stalls are set up in the streets that tower with carvings made out of the red-and-white vegetables. They depict scenes with Christmas themes and figures of animals, kings, or mariachi (Mexican musicians). When the Spanish brought radishes to Mexico four hundred years ago, they found it impossible to persuade the local population to cultivate them. It was only the Dominican friars who managed it. When the farmers were gathering their crops, one of the friars suggested carving shapes out of the radishes. "People will be happy to buy such pretty vegetables," he said to convince them. And indeed, the farmers sold every last one of their radishes. Ever since, a competition has been held for the most interesting radish sculpture.

Silent night

"Silent night, holy night" goes the familiar Christmas carol. In Poland Christmas Eve is when the main festive meal takes place. In the Polish language, the name of this special night is Wigilia, which means "the vigil." It comes from the Latin word *vigilare*, meaning "to be on watch, to be prepared"—because this is the night when we eagerly await the birth of the most wonderful child in the world.

In Poland the traditional Wigilia super is a Lenten meal, which means it doesn't include meat though it does include fish—the main dish is carp. In Germany there are sausages and roast goose on the table too. In Great Britain the main dish for the traditional Christmas lunch (eaten on Christmas Day) is roast turkey. In the United States, the Christmas Day feast is often roast turkey, ham, or roast beef. (You'll find more about Christmas dishes on page 78). In Belgium Christmas Eve is celebrated by families and friends who meet together at restaurants.

In just a few countries, including Poland and Sweden, the children are given their presents on Christmas Eve. Most children have to wait until the next day, as in the United States, for instance, or even longer—in Spain they don't receive them until January 6.

Only one thing is exactly the same in most countries, and that's Midnight Mass. It's held on the night of December 24 to 25, and it's also known as the "shepherds' mass" because of the shepherds who, on hearing of the birth of Jesus Christ, fell to their knees in ardent prayer and gave thanks for the new God. Only the Spanish have a different name for this mass: Misa de Gallo, which means "the rooster's mass," probably because it's the first event of the new day, like the crowing of a rooster.

The residents of Caracas in Venezuela go to Midnight Mass on rollerblades or roller skates. So many people are eager to go that the streets in the city center are closed to cars on that night. Nobody knows exactly how this tradition originated. Some suppose it was out of envy for sleighs, because the Venezuelans can't expect any snow at Christmas so they won't be traveling by sled. That's why they chose such an unusual form of transport for the festive season.

A mysterious light

According to tradition, the Poles cannot sit down to their Wigilia supper until the first star begins to shine. That was the sign that is said to have appeared in the sky when Jesus was born in the stable in Bethlehem.

The Bible suggests that this star, known as the Star of Bethlehem, slowly changed position, showing the three kings (see page 120) the way to the Holy Infant. For many years experts on the Bible, astronomers, and other scholars have wondered what light it was that guided the wise men to Bethlehem. Is the Star of Bethlehem just a legend or was there really an unusual astronomical occurrence two thousand years ago? They take several possibilities into consideration.

For instance, they suspect that the Star of Bethlehem might have been a comet with a glowing tail. In the old chronicles they have found information to say that a celestial body was seen shining in the sky for nearly a month; alarmed by this sight, people ascribed magical powers to it.

The unusual phenomenon could also have been caused by the eruption of a supernova, which is a star that ends its life with a spectacular explosion. Surrounded by a cloud of gases and dust, a star of this kind is visible in the daytime as well as at night.

Finally, the scientists speculate that at the time when Jesus was born, several planets (including possibly Jupiter, Saturn, Venus, and Mars) were positioned in a single line. They weren't shielding one another, but on the contrary, their light merged to produce a brightly shining object in the sky. As in astrology, Jupiter symbolizes power, spirituality, and strength; the three kings could have interpreted this marvel as a sign marking the birth of an unusual person.

Nor do the scholars exclude the possibility that a series of remarkable events occurred within a short period of time and confirmed people in the belief that something important was about to happen.

How to be sure of good luck

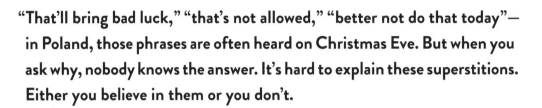

"That'll bring bad luck," "that's not allowed," "better not do that today"— in Poland, those phrases are often heard on Christmas Eve. But when you ask why, nobody knows the answer. It's hard to explain these superstitions. Either you believe in them or you don't.

Many of the superstitions (or beliefs that have no real foundation) associated with Wigilia, the Polish Christmas celebration, came from the conviction that people should behave just as well throughout the year as on this very special day. And so, on this exceptional night, you shouldn't argue or scheme (or you'll do it all year long), and you're not allowed to lend anything (because if you never stop giving, you'll be in need yourself).

The superstitions are often about what to do, and what not to do, to be sure of good luck. Apparently, the first person to cross the threshold on Wigilia night has to be a man, because a woman will bring bad luck. You'll also have misfortune if the number of places at the table isn't even. To make sure, it's better to add an extra place. It doesn't matter if there's no one sitting there—we don't argue with superstitions!

It's hard to explain superstitions rationally, and yet many people carry out these recommendations without batting an eyelid. For example, the suggestion is that you must be sure to put a scale from the Wigilia carp into your wallet because then you'll have lots of money. It doesn't sound logical, does it? And yet in Poland people do it because you never know. Some people also put coins under their plates to guarantee themselves wealth. Or they hide a coin inside a dumpling that's added to the soup—just to be on the safe side. But be careful not to break your teeth on it!

In Silesia and Slovakia there's a superstition that doesn't quite tally with tradition. According to custom, if a lost wanderer knocks at the door, you should welcome the person, but according to superstition, you're not supposed to stand up from the table during the Wigilia supper for any reason whatsoever because that will bring bad luck. So how are we to reconcile it all?

It's not just the Poles who believe in Christmas Eve superstitions. On that day the Norwegians carefully hide all their brooms, brushes, and mops in the closet. Why is that? Because they believe that on Christmas Eve witches appear in the houses looking for something on which they can fly. And naturally nobody wants to be robbed of such a useful household object.

An extra place for an unexpected guest

At Christmas nobody should be alone. In some countries, in case someone knocks at the door and asks for shelter, an extra place is laid at the Christmas table.

When Mary and Joseph arrived in Bethlehem, they knocked at the doors of houses, asking for shelter for the night, but nobody was willing to take them in. Then, in an out-of-the-way place, Joseph found a deserted cave—or in other versions, a stable. That night Jesus was born. Some people say it's because of this story that it's customary to lay an extra place at the Christmas table for an unexpected guest. The empty plate is there to remind us that on this night no one can refuse hospitality.

But there's another explanation for this tradition too. In the past, an extra place at the table was left for relatives who had died (this custom is still practiced in some parts of Ukraine) in the belief that on Christmas Eve they visited their families as ghosts. When the supper came to an end, the householders did not clear the table but left the remains of the food on it. Once everyone had gone to bed, the ghosts could eat and drink without fear of being disturbed by anyone. To this day, an extra place reminds many people of their loved ones who have passed on. Or of those who are alive but for some reason cannot spend Christmas with their family.

Straight from the meadow

It's hidden under the tablecloth during the Christmas meal, and you can use it to predict the future. What is it? A piece of hay! Here's another Polish tradition with an interesting origin.

The explanation is simple. Jesus was born in a cave, or as tradition prefers, in a stable. In the past, animals lived in the same space as people. Mary and Joseph were poor. They had no cradle, so they wrapped the Holy Infant in a cloth and laid him in a manger. But what was lining the manger? Not soft bedding, unfortunately, but what horses and cows eat: hay. That's why meadow grasses harvested in the spring have appeared in festively decorated homes for centuries as a reminder of the miraculous birth of Christ in Bethlehem. People used to stack entire sheaves of hay in the corners of their rooms. After Christmas the hay was woven into strings that were tied around the trees in the orchard in the hope that they'd produce plenty of fruit that summer.

According to an old custom, the young women drew single blades of hay from under the tablecloth to find out what fate lay ahead of them. If a girl drew a green blade, it meant her wedding would take place soon; if she drew a wilting blade, it meant she'd have to wait a bit longer for her beloved; and if she drew a yellow blade, she'd never be married.

Nowadays the hay doesn't necessarily have to be hidden under the tablecloth. Some people put it on a small plate, while others scatter it on the cloth in the middle of the table and stand the serving dishes on it. You can also make straw figures out of it and stand them on the plates so that each guest is given his or her own miniature sheaf. What does your imagination suggest?

Let's share

It doesn't look like much—just a small, thin sheet made of flour and water. But in Polish tradition, the Christmas wafer is something important and special that people share while exchanging their best wishes for good luck and love.

The custom of breaking the wafer during the Wigilia Christmas Eve supper is only familiar in a few countries around the world.

The Polish wafer looks like a semitransparent piece of tissue paper. It's made of nothing but flour and water. The supple dough is similar to the kind used to make pancakes. You spread it at the bottom of a special mold that looks like a waffle maker. Then you close the lid, which has a decorative pattern engraved on it (showing the Holy Family in the stable, for example), and you wait for the result. At first the wafer is a yellowish shade, but a month later it acquires its familiar white color (though there are also colored wafers, green and pink, which people in the countryside share with their animals). Even if you keep the wafers for a long time, they stay fresh, so you can bake them all year round.

In the late-eighteenth century, when Poland lost its independence and was divided up between three empires, the Poles suddenly became citizens of different countries. But they wanted to stay in touch and to keep their traditions alive at any price. And so they sent one another wafers in letters during the Christmas season. This was their symbolic way of comforting

their loved ones and expressing the fact that nobody and nothing could keep them apart. Nowadays the Poles can send their families and friends ready-made cards that include wafers.

In the past the wafer wasn't just for sharing. It was a snack for the adults to eat while drinking wine. Coated in honey, it was a favorite treat for the children. In aristocratic homes it was also used to seal letters. And finally, Christmas decorations were cut out of wafers in the shape of little crosses, suns, and stars. The more artistic people crafted cradles for the Holy Infant by sticking the pieces of wafers together with saliva or made intricate three-dimensional decorations that were ball shaped and could be hung from the roof beams.

But Christmas wafers don't look the same everywhere. In Russian Orthodox countries (see page 128), including Ukraine and Belarus, the wafer is nothing other than a traditional kind of bread (called an *oplatek*, a word that comes from the Latin *oblata*, meaning a ritual loaf). It is made of flour, water, salt, and a leavening agent. It's quite small, and it consists of two rings, one bigger than the other. The smaller one usually has the shape of a cross stamped on it. The Orthodox wafer is known as a *prosphoron*. Those taking part in the Christmas Eve celebratory supper eat it piece by piece while sipping consecrated water.

In Greece the wafer is also a kind of bread, but it's called *christopsomo*, which literally means "Christ's bread." Before it's cut into pieces and distributed to

the householders, the head of the family holds the loaf above the fire and pours olive oil or wine over it.

Matters are entirely different in Spain because there the wafer is like a . . . . candy bar. It is nothing more or less than a piece of sweet nougat made of honey, sugar, almonds, pine nuts, and hazelnuts. The Spanish call it *turrón*. It can be hard or a little softer, like fudge. It is cut into small pieces and handed out to all members of the family. The Spanish can't imagine a Christmas Eve supper without it. In the town of Jijona there's even a museum dedicated to this kind of Christmas wafer.

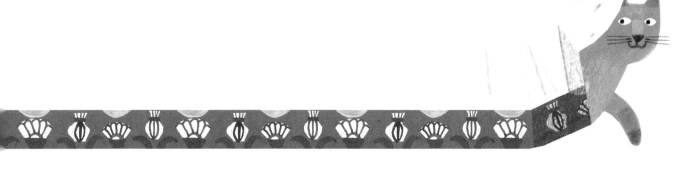

The festive dozen

Fish, pierogi, cabbage, beet soup, noodles with poppy seeds, fruit compote — what a lot of food! And what's more, you have to try each one. In Poland, why do the grown-ups think it's so important to have as many as twelve different dishes on the festive table?

According to popular custom, there should be as many dishes as there are months in the year. The belief is that if you try each of the twelve dishes, you won't suffer from hunger for a single month in the year ahead. But there's another theory too, which is that the number *12* refers to the twelve apostles, Jesus's disciples, who after his death traveled the world preaching the new faith.

Beet soup with
dumplings

Lingonberry water

Beet salad

Baked carp

Pickled herrings

As well as the correct number, the Polish Christmas dishes should meet one other condition too: they should consist of foods harvested from the fields (so there are dishes made of flour, buckwheat, and poppy seed), the orchards (dried fruits, nuts, and honey), the forests (mushrooms), and the ponds (fish). In the past, magical properties were ascribed to each ingredient: for example, nuts provided physical strength and wisdom while mushrooms, regarded as unusual because they come from the deep, dark forest, guaranteed control over supernatural powers. Poppy seed was an especially important item, a symbol of prosperity and wealth. Did you know that in days of old it was used to make a hallucinogenic infusion that caused mild intoxication and drowsiness? Nowadays we also know that it has a relaxing effect and helps you to sleep better. But don't fall asleep until you've tried all twelve of the Christmas dishes!

Cabbage with mushrooms

Greek-style fish

Fish in aspic

Poppyseed cakes

Dried fruit compote

Bread

Pierogi with mushroom filling

Some mouth-watering treats

The dishes served for the Polish Christmas Eve supper are Lenten, in other words, without meat. The Poles don't eat any cooked meats until Christmas Day. But what dishes are people eating in other parts of the world at this time of year? Here are some of the most interesting.

Kutia—this is from the Greek word *kókkos*, meaning "pip" or "seed"; this dish is made of wheat, poppy seeds, raisins, nuts, and honey, which holds all the other ingredients together. It's popular in Ukraine, Lithuania, and Russia, and also in Poland.

Lutefisk—this means "soapy fish"; it's a Norwegian dish, and you have to start preparing it about two weeks before the holiday. You soak some dried cod in water for several days, then in lye (an extremely caustic substance). In the process, the fish gains a jellylike consistency. Then you have to rinse it entirely clean of lye before boiling or frying it. It's served with vegetables.

Jansson's Temptation—this is a sort of Swedish pizza made with potatoes, onions, and sprats or anchovies, with the addition of sour cream and white pepper. Apparently, it owes its name to a Swedish opera singer named Per Adolf Janzon, who lived more

Glögg

Julskinka

than 130 years ago. He was the son of a fishmonger, and whenever he invited guests for supper, he always served them a fish dish of this kind.

Julskinka—this is Swedish Christmas ham in a honey-mustard crust, boiled in broth and then baked in the oven. It's the main dish served at the Swedish Christmas Eve feast. Traditionally, before everyone gets to taste it, they eat bread dipped in the stock in which it was boiled. That's what the children from the village of Bullerby did as they waited for the Jultomtar (Santa's elves) to arrive in the famous children's book by Astrid Lindgren *The Children of Noisy Village*.

Glögg—this is wine heated with orange peel, cinnamon, cardamom, cloves, and ginger, popular in all the Scandinavian countries. The name is derived from the old Swedish word *glöd*, meaning "heat." There's also a nonalcoholic version of this drink made with fruit and chocolate.

Bûche de Noël—translated literally, this means "Christmas log"; it's a French cake shaped like a log: a sponge roll filled with cream flavored with vanilla, coffee, or walnuts and coated in chocolate, often decorated with real sprigs of spruce and pinecones. How do we explain the unusual shape of this cake? Perhaps the French housekeepers were inspired by the old custom, according to which the head of the family brought home a large log on Christmas Eve, sprinkled it with olive oil or wine, and then tossed it into the fireplace. The family then sat by the fire awaiting the arrival of Jesus. Traditionally, this cake is served after Midnight Mass (see page 64).

Jansson's Temptation

Eggnog—this is a hot, very sweet American drink made with raw egg yolks and milk, seasoned with vanilla, cinnamon, honey, and nutmeg. It's similar to kogel mogel (an egg-based dessert popular in parts of Europe).

Hallaca—this is a Venezuelan snack. It's made of cooked chicken, beef, or pork, with some cheese, olives, capers, and raisins added to it. It is wrapped in corn-flour pastry and then banana leaves. The parcels are boiled in a pot, and then the leaves are peeled off and unwrapped like Christmas presents like Christmas presents.

Kourabiedes—these are Greek butter cookies rolled in powdered sugar. They're made of shortbread pastry combined with crushed almonds and sprinkled with rose water.

Christmas pudding—this is a British dish, and you start preparing it in September. You combine thirteen ingredients in a bowl (in honor of Jesus and the twelve apostles), including flour, sugar, eggs, animal fat, nuts and dried fruit, candied cherries, rum, and seasoning. According to tradition, each member of the family mixes the ingredients with a wooden spoon, from east to west. The mixture is wrapped in a cotton cloth and set aside in a cool spot. Once a week the pudding is taken out, mixed again, and set aside. Just before Christmas it's boiled for about two hours. It is brought to the Christmas table coated in hot, flaming rum.

Eggnog

Hallaca

Kourabiedes

Panettone and **pandoro**—these are traditional Italian cakes. Panettone comes from Milan and pandoro from Verona. Panettone is shaped like a dome and contains lots of dried fruit and nuts. Traditionally it should be prepared and baked for sixty hours; then it should hang upside down for another ten hours to acquire the right shape. The Italian word *panettone* means "big bread." But there's another explanation for the origin of this name too: One day a feast was being held at the court of Ludovico Sforza, the duke of Milan. The main dessert was just about to be brought to the table when a tragedy occurred! The cake burned, and there was panic in the kitchen. But then the chef's assistant, whose name was Toni, baked a new cake, which was an instant hit with the duke's grand guests. That was how il pan di Toni—Toni's bread, or rather panettone—was born.

Pandoro doesn't contain any dried fruit or nuts, but it's coated in icing or a sprinkling of powdered sugar. Its base is shaped like an eight-point star, and it's golden-yellow inside; the Italian word for *gold* is *oro*, hence its name, *pandoro*: golden bread.

Christmas pudding

Panettone

Pandoro

Bûche de Noël

Let us sing for the Christ Child!

Every year people come from all over the world to the town of Oberndorf bei Salzburg in Austria at exactly 5:00 p.m. to sing "Silent Night," one of the most beautiful Christmas carols.

The young priest Joseph Mohr didn't think of himself as a poet, and his friend, the organist Franz Gruber, was not a composer; but together they created a song that very soon became the most famous Christmas carol in the world. The year was 1818, and it was early afternoon on December 24. In the town of Oberndorf bei Salzburg the snow was falling, and the frost was biting. Father Joseph was walking along the deserted streets holding a scroll of paper with something written on it. He couldn't stop thinking about the touching scene he'd witnessed two years earlier in another parish when he'd paid a visit to a woman who had recently given birth. The home was very poor, but the new parents' joy was indescribable. The young priest had been extremely moved by this encounter, and as soon as he returned to the presbytery, he'd written a poem. He thought it was quite good, but so far he hadn't had the courage to show it to anyone. Now he had finally decided to show off his work. So he went to see his friend the organist to ask him to compose some music for his short text. As luck would have it, the organ was in need of repair, so the friends accompanied each other on guitars. Gruber wrote the music in just a few hours. That same night, at Midnight Mass in the church of Saint Nicholas, they performed the carol, and everyone fell in love with it.

Today, at the site of that church, on a small hill there's a chapel surrounded by fir trees. There are some steps leading up to it, illuminated by two atmospheric lamps. Inside there are stained-glass windows. One depicts Franz Gruber holding a guitar, and the other shows Joseph Mohr with a goose quill and a sheet of paper. On Christmas Eve, the Silent Night chapel, usually isolated and forgotten, is at the center of attention. Every year crowds of people gather below it to listen, just before dusk, as two soloists and a choir perform the carol "Silent Night". And then they sing it together in various languages.

Curiously, in the past carols weren't associated with Christmas at all. In Greece they're called *kalanda*, and in Polish *kolędy*, words that come from the Latin *calendae*, or "calends," meaning the first day of the month; and that's because songs of this kind were performed at New Year's, on the first day of January. In Poland they were sung by men and women dressed up as the devil, a shepherd, an angel, and the wicked King Herod. The singers often shielded their faces with masks representing a sheep, a goat, or a *turoń*: a black monster that snapped its jaws. Usually, one of the men carried a star made of brightly colored paper.

These mummers went from house to house wishing the residents good fortune. They prepared special shows known as "Herod plays," which told the story of the evil King Herod, who tried to kill the baby Jesus. The mummers often played tricks on people too, covering them in soot, for instance. Like magic spells, their songs were meant to bring their hosts good luck and a bountiful harvest. But of course there was a condition: their hosts had to thank them with gifts in the form of food or small coins.

Polish carols also include a kind of song called a *pastorałka*. It tells the story of the birth of Jesus too, but it's not as solemn as most carols—instead it's lighter and jollier. It's often a shepherds' folk song sung in a local dialect.

Say something!

They say that at midnight on Christmas Eve animals speak in human voices. What's the origin of this belief?

Of course, you can't expect to hear a canary or a guinea pig talking like a person. Only the animals that were with the Holy Family in the stable when Jesus was born are going to speak: cows, horses, sheep, and goats. And cats and dogs too, because they're always roaming around somewhere nearby. And maybe mice too, because they are often to be found hiding in hay. The old belief was that these creatures were the first to meow, bleat, and bark the good news. Maybe that's why rural people still share their Christmas wafers (see page 74) with them to this day.

But what do they say to us at midnight? Some people claim the ghosts of our ancestors appear on Christmas Eve and talk through them. Others think it's better not to listen to what the animals say, because they can foretell how long we're going to live. Whatever the case, they're sure to speak the truth, because animals don't know how to lie like people. And watch out if you haven't always been kind to them—they're sure to tell you off!

But do you really have to wait until Christmas Eve to have a conversation with the dog?

From the biological point of view, a dog's or a cat's vocal apparatus isn't all that different from the human kind, so animals could talk, if not for the fact that they're not able to put their thoughts into words. But that doesn't stop them from communicating with us. They do it with body language, by wagging their tails, putting out their tongues, or resting their snouts on our knees.

What does Santa Claus look like?

That's easy—he's an old man dressed in a red coat and hat. And he has a long white beard. But did you know that he hasn't always been imagined that way?

At first he was thought to look like a bishop, Saint Nicholas of Myra, wearing a distinctive miter (a triangular hat) and holding a crosier (a long, decorated staff with a curled top shaped like a snail shell). That's how the Russians imagine him to this day. Or else they think he resembles a gnome. In the early-nineteenth century, the writer Clement Clarke Moore described him in a poem as looking like an elf riding around in a miniature sleigh harnessed to tiny reindeer.

It all changed in 1931. The American illustrator Haddon Sundblom was given the task of drawing Santa Claus for a Christmas advertisement for Coca-Cola. Sundblom depicted the saint as a plump, jovial old man with a long white beard and ruddy cheeks, dressed in a red coat, red pants, and red hat. In fact, he made Santa Claus look quite like himself. The jolly old fellow immediately conquered the hearts of children the world over. Ever since, that's how we usually imagine him.

1956 December

S M T W TH Fr S
1
2 3 4 5 6 7 8
9 10 11 12 13 14 15
16 17 18 19 20 21 22
23 24 25 26 27 28 29
30 31

Santa Claus is often shown in the company of his trusty helpers. For example, in Great Britain the saint's entourage includes a mischievous imp named Jack Frost, who draws crystal flowers on the windows. In America Santa's retinue consists of elves in short green jackets and caps, and in Russia he's helped by his granddaughter, Snegurochka (the Snow Maiden).

It's different in the Alpine countries, such as Austria and Germany. Here the benevolent Santa is followed by processions of devils, with horns, long white beards, and fangs. They're dressed in fur coats, and their faces are hidden behind terrifying masks carved out of wood. They're known as Krampus, and they aren't there to help the saint at all—on the contrary, they do all they can to spoil his meetings with the children. They howl, roar, crack whips, rattle chains, and jangle little cow bells attached to their belts. They scare the passers-by, stealing their hats and scarves, and sometimes lashing at people's legs with birch twigs. Luckily the Einspieler is always close by—an elegant gentleman in a tail coat, top hat, and tall boots who keeps order. If one of the Krampus

figures is causing too much trouble, the Einspieler restrains him by striking him on the horns with his cane.

Curiously, in Greece Saint Nicholas is not associated with presents. The Greeks see him as the patron saint of sailors and fishermen.

In most countries Santa Claus comes twice—first on Saint Nicholas's Day and then at Christmas. In Poland, Chile, and Denmark he visits the children on Christmas Eve. In America, Great Britain, Italy, Germany, France, the Netherlands, and Belgium he appears on December 25. And in Russia he doesn't arrive until January 1.

Who delivers the presents?

Do you think it's just an old guy dressed in red who delivers the presents? You'll be amazed to find out that in some countries it's a privilege enjoyed by someone else entirely.

Elves. They look quite like Santa, but in miniature. For example, in Sweden the gifts are distributed on Christmas Eve by the Jultomtar, a bit like garden gnomes who ride in a sleigh pulled by a goat.

And then in Iceland thirteen elves known as the Jólasveinar come to the children. They haven't always been friendly—in the past they were more like horrid little trolls. Thirteen days before Christmas, one after another they used to come down from high in the mountains to play tricks on people. They'd rampage around their farms, destroying supplies and tools. For instance, the Sheep Scarer had wooden legs and stole sheep's milk. The Gully Gawk

frightened cows, causing their milk to dry up, and the Door Slammer made a monstrous racket. On December 25, suddenly, one after another they would start to go away. They went back into the mountains and didn't appear again for another year. Nowadays they are better behaved, and instead of making people's lives miserable, they tell them fairy tales and sing songs. By turns, each of them puts one small gift into children's shoes for thirteen days. And at the very worst, pilfers a candle or a sausage.

The Infant Jesus. In Silesia, Austria, and Germany (in the southern and eastern regions), instead of a messenger such as Santa Claus, the presents are brought by God himself, in the form of the baby Jesus. He appears on Christmas Eve.

The Starman (Gwiazdor). He can be frightening! He's an old man dressed in a long sheepskin coat and a fur hat. His face is hidden behind a mask. He has a sack full of presents on his back, and he's holding a star (hence his name) and a switch to scold the bad children who don't deserve presents. On Christmas Eve he comes to the Polish children in Kujawy, Kashubia, Lubuskie, and the Poznań region. He's more and more often replaced by Santa Claus.

Saint Basil (Agios Vasilis). He delivers the presents in Greece. He appears on the night of December 31 to January 1. When midnight strikes, the head of the family cuts a Saint Basil's cake, made specially for this day, called a vasilopita, with a coin hidden inside it. That's a memento of a particular legend: One day, to protect his city from enemy attack, Bishop Vasilis (or Basil) decided to pay off the enemy, so he organized a collection of money from all the residents. But meanwhile the enemy troops withdrew from their siege without taking the payment. So Saint Basil gave the people back their money, but in an unusual way: He had round loaves baked with coins and small gifts inside. Then he went into the city and while issuing blessings, handed out the bread rolls. How happy the residents were when they cut the bread and found a surprise inside it!

Los Reyes Magos. That's the Spanish name for the three kings. They bring presents for the Spanish children on January 6. Of course, sometimes the children are also given some small gifts earlier, on December 25, but they only receive their main presents in January.

El Olentzero or **el Onentzaro**. A farmer or miner who on December 25 hands out the presents in the Basque Country, a region in the north of Spain at the foot of the Pyrenees. He's a friendly, chubby fellow dressed in a Basque beret, a peasant costume, and distinctive shoes called *abarketak* tied with strings above the ankle. His name comes from the Basque words *onen (good)* and *zaro (time)*, which can be translated as "time of good." That's what the Christmas season used to be called in the Basque Country.

A visit to Santa

For six months of the year the sun doesn't set there, and for the other six it's as dark as night. Endless snowy plains stretch in all directions. This truly magical landscape is in Lapland, northern Finland. Just beyond the Arctic Circle, five miles from the city of Rovaniemi—that's where Santa Claus lives.

Santa Claus visits the children in December, but the children can go and visit him on any day of the year at his village beyond the Arctic Circle. The best time to do that is in the summer when he's not so busy. Above the entrance to his house there's a clock that shows if Santa can see you now or if he's having a nap. The smiling old man with a long beard receives his visitors in a large hall, sitting on a solid oak chair that stands on a podium so that everyone has a good view of him. Each visitor can go up to him, exchange a few words with him, and take a souvenir photo. Then the visitor can tour the village: the post office where the trusty elves sort the correspondence that comes from all over the world, the famous sleigh in which Santa travels at Christmas, and the enclosure where his most loyal helper lives—the reindeer (if you wish, you can go on a ride in a vehicle pulled by him). Nearby there's also SantaPark, where you can see the Elf School and Mrs. Gingerbread's Bakery. When you feel hungry, you can go to a restaurant there serving Finnish specialties. And if your tour lasts until late in the evening, you can stay the night at a hotel in the village.

Don't worry if you can't go visit Santa Claus in person. Take a look at his online TV channel (santatelevision.com), where you can watch him getting ready for his Christmas journey, inspecting his sleigh, and picking blueberries in the forest. And you can write to Santa—why not send him a letter? Here's his address: Santa Claus Office, Tähtikuja 1, 96930 Rovaniemi, Finland, or email: joulupukinpaaposti@posti.fi.

A fast-food supper

Although the most important religion in Japan is Buddhism, many Japanese people celebrate the Christian Christmas. Here's how they do it.

The Japanese are famous for being open to other cultures and for borrowing whatever they like from them. And so it is with Christmas. Toward the end of November, the Japanese streets twinkle with Christmas illuminations, and the store assistants welcome their customers by greeting them in English: "Merry Christmas!" There's a Christmas tree in every home and numerous figurines representing Santa Claus, his reindeer, and ... panda bears! Friends send one another Christmas cards with pictures of angels, snow-coated towns, and children singing carols.

The Japanese name for Christmas is Kurisumasu, but they don't regard it as a religious holiday. And on December 24, 25, and 26 they still go to work. On Christmas Eve, instead of staying at home, they all go out to restaurants. But guess what kind? They go to the American fast-food chain KFC. Yes, that's right! The Japanese are crazy about chicken, and no one's surprised to see crowds of people eating fried chicken in a spicy batter on Christmas Eve. On that one evening KFC makes more money than in several months! Oh well, every country has its special customs.

Japanese Christmas Eve is an excuse to invite your girlfriend out for a very special dinner and to propose to her—in the last few years Kurisumasu has become the second most important holiday for lovers after Saint Valentine's Day. On that day it's hard to find a free table at a restaurant if you haven't booked in advance.

What do we do at Christmas?

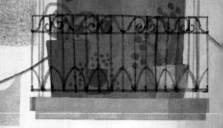

What's your first thought? We do a lot of eating and gift giving. But Christmas isn't limited just to feasting. How do people spend Christmas around the world?

Having fun. When it strikes midnight on Christmas Eve, the inhabitants of South America run outside to offer their best wishes to their neighbors, and then they party until dawn. In Argentina, just before Midnight Mass the sky is lit up by fireworks, and then hundreds of paper lanterns fly toward the stars.

Playing sports. To drop the extra pounds gained at Christmas, on December 26 in Prague, capital of the Czech Republic, winter-bathing enthusiasts (known as walruses) meet up to plunge into the icy waters of the Vltava River. At the same time, in Australia and New Zealand it's high summer—so the people of those countries celebrate Christmas on the beach, surfing or playing volleyball.

The Italians are also seasoned players, but the sport they enjoy doesn't demand physical fitness, because the Italians are passionate card players. Each region has its own special deck—in the north they use the so-called Piacentine, and in Naples it's the *abido*, which instead of the familiar suits—spades, hearts, diamonds, and clubs—have swords, cups, cudgels, and coins. Board games are popular too—the Italians are particularly fond of one named Tombola, which is similar to bingo.

Shopping. When December 26 comes, the Irish and the British flock in large crowds to all the shopping malls, because on that day (known as Boxing Day) the Christmas sales begin. Physical fitness is very useful—fast reflexes and speedy legs guarantee that the shoppers won't miss a single bargain. Shopping after Christmas at reduced prices is also very popular in Poland.

April Fool's Day in December

If you happen to be in Spain, Colombia, or Mexico on December 28, be on your guard, because that's when everyone plays tricks and tells tall stories.

There are traps everywhere: the television broadcasts made-up news, and the waiter serves coffee with salt instead of sugar. It's the Day of the Holy Innocents, the local equivalent of April Fool's Day. Everyone's in a very jolly mood, though in fact this holiday commemorates a sad event.

As it says in the Bible, when Jesus was born, Judea was ruled by the cruel King Herod. When he heard that a future king had been born in a stable in Bethlehem who, according to prophecy, would be mightier than all the rulers on Earth, out of envy Herod decided to kill him. But he didn't know where he was hiding, so he gave an order for all the newborn male babies in the kingdom to be killed. Luckily, Joseph, Mary, and the baby Jesus managed to escape the rage of the heartless king in time.

The residents of Venezuela celebrate April Fool's Day on December 28 too, but they call their holiday the Fiesta de Locos, meaning "Feast of Fools"—because Herod must have been crazy to issue such a merciless order. On that day, in many Venezuelan towns and villages there are parades of clowns and oddballs, demons and freaks. In the state of Lara the parade also features dancers known as *zaragozas*—men and boys dressed in women's clothes, trimmed with ribbons, bows, and bells. The zaragozas talk in shrill voices so that no one will recognize them, and they dance to the beat of the Venezuelan folk dance the *tamunangue*.

The Nutcracker and the Mouse King

When the Christmas tree was decorated with walnuts, there had to be a nutcracker on the festive table. And there's a Christmas legend about it.

Apparently, nutcrackers were first invented in Germany. A burgher (meaning a privileged resident) who was tired of constantly having to crush walnuts in his hands decided to find another way to extract the delicious nuts from their shells. His friend who was a carpenter advised him to cut the shells with a saw, his friend who was a soldier suggested shooting at them, and his puppet-maker friend said he should carve a wooden figure to crush the walnuts in its jaws. The burgher liked the third idea, and that's how nutcrackers came to be. Originally, they were in the shape of a soldier, a king, or a drummer boy; you pulled on the back of his wig to open his jaws wide, and then he crushed the walnut.

There's a grain of truth in every legend—of course, a device for shelling nuts had been invented long before that, but it was only thanks to the German puppet-makers that the object started to look like a soldier. It was also in Germany that the beautiful fairy tale about the Nutcracker was created.

The story begins on Christmas Eve. Herr Drosselmeyer, the judge, calls at the home of Councilor Stahlbaum to present his godchildren, Clara and Fritz, with gifts that he has made for them himself as he does every year. This time as well as a beautiful palace with mechanical figures, he gives Klara something else: a little wooden figure with a large head and moving jaws. That night the Nutcracker takes Clara to an enchanted land, where there'll be a fight to the death with the terrible Mouse King.

The story was written by the German author E T. A. Hoffmann, but it was made more famous by the ballet that was based on it. The music for the ballet was composed by Pyotr Ilyich Tchaikovsky. You can see a performance of it every year in the Christmas season at various opera houses.

Did you know that the famous story about the Nutcracker originated in Poland? The author's wife was Polish, and he used to spend time in the Polish cities of Poznań, Płock, and Warsaw. In Warsaw he often visited his good friends the Hitzig family who lived in a house on Freta Street. Apparently that was where he first had the idea for the story. Hoffmann was inspired by Mr. and Mrs. Hitzig's children, Maria and Fritz, who were the models for the brother and sister in the story.

One of the most famous scenes in ballet is from *The Nutcracker*, and it's called The Dance of the Sugar-Plum Fairy. Every ballerina dreams of performing this dance one day.

The ghosts of Christmas

The festive season is a time when people are nicer to one another. And that was even true of a mean, unlovable old man named Scrooge.

There's probably never been a crabbier old man than Ebenezer Scrooge. He wouldn't talk to anyone, and his answer to every greeting was just a nasty growl; he treated his employee badly and avoided his relatives like wildfire. The only thing that mattered in his life was money. Nothing else pleased him, and he seemed to love it more than he liked people. Everyone gave him a wide berth because they knew they could only expect unpleasantness from him.

Until one night on Christmas Eve when Scrooge came home and sat down as usual in his old armchair. The ghost of his deceased business partner, Jacob Marley, appeared to him. Like Scrooge he had been a miser and now, after his death, was suffering torment in hell as a result. That night Scrooge was haunted by three more ghosts. They showed him scenes from his life—past, present, and future. Did these visitations cause Scrooge to change his ways? You can read the story in one of the most famous books in the world, *A Christmas Carol*, by Charles Dickens. Dickens wrote the story to pay off his debts and never expected it to be such a huge success. To this day the book is extremely popular, and several movies and animated films have been made of it.

Ebenezer Scrooge was a real person, but he wasn't a miser at all. His actual name was Ebenezer Lennox Scroggie, and he traded in corn and wine. Dickens happened to come upon his tombstone in a graveyard in Edinburgh and mistakenly took him to be a miser. The inscription on his tombstone said he was a "meal man," which means someone who trades in grain; but Dickens read it wrongly as a "mean man." He was so moved by it that he came up with the idea of writing the book. What on earth would Mr. Scroggie have had to say? Perhaps he wouldn't have been terribly annoyed if he'd known that he'd accidentally become the hero of a famous story.

A Christmas Carol was written in only six weeks! It appeared in the bookstores just before Christmas, on December 19, 1843. The first edition was sold out in a few days!

At midnight

On the night of December 31 to January 1, there's no question of going to bed. That's when champagne corks shoot into the air, and the sky is lit up by fireworks. Most people around the world celebrate New Year's Eve.

In ancient times the Greek soothsayer, the Sybil, is said to have predicted that on the night of December 31, 999, to January 1, 1000, the world would come to an end. That night the monster Leviathan, imprisoned in the dungeons of the Vatican, would awake and destroy everything. When the time was approaching, the reigning pope in Rome was Sylvester II. All Europe tensely awaited that night. Some people hid away in their houses, while others gathered in the churches to pray; but when midnight struck, the monster didn't appear, and life carried on as if nothing had happened. So the people ran out into the streets to celebrate the arrival of the new year. They sang and danced until dawn. Pope Sylvester II breathed a sigh of relief too and joyfully appeared in the windows of his palace. He greeted the people cheering in the streets and wished them every good fortune. Ever since, in some countries the night from December to January has been named after the pope: Silvester's night. And although nowadays nobody believes the end of the world is at hand, everyone's very pleased when the clocks strike midnight.

Long ago the new year was not celebrated in January but with the coming of spring. That was when the ancient Greeks held a festival called the Dionysia, in honor of Dionysus, the god of the grape harvest. They paraded in a jolly procession, carrying baskets with newborn babies lying in them. The infants symbolized the start of something new. To this day, in Iran and Thailand, grand celebrations are held from late March to early April.

In China, according to the traditional calendar, the new year comes at the turn of January and February.

New Year double celebration

In Switzerland or, to be more precise, in the canton of Appenzell Ausserrhoden, the New Year is celebrated twice. In addition to December 31 the bells ring on January 13. This is because, according to the old Julian calendar, New Year's Eve is on that date. And so the good folk of Appenzell simply enjoy two parties.

It's an ancient custom that on both days the Silvesterchläuse make their appearance. These are people dressed up in one of three disguises: the *Schöne* (beautiful), the *Schö-Wüeschte* (beautiful-ugly), and the *Wüeschte* (ugly).

They're all fascinating to look at in their lavish costumes of branches and handmade decorations.

The Schöne wear ornate headdresses—handmade over many hours—depicting scenes from rural life. The Schö-Wüeschte and the Wüeschte wear a striking array of crazy hats and masks.

Before you see them, you can hear them from far away. They have large bells hanging from their bodies. They go from one farm to another in small groups, bringing New Year greetings and good wishes to all the families. They sing at the top of their voices and ring their bells. The audience—which includes lots of visitors and tourists—watch and listen as this unique spectacle unfolds. The Silvesterchlause really seem like creatures from another planet.

For the performers, this is a physically demanding exercise. The costumes can weigh between 44–66 pounds (20 and 30 kilograms), and the celebrations go on all day in Appenzell Ausserrhoden. The procession begins early in the morning and often goes on until midnight or later, when the costumed revellers end up visiting the pubs.

For good luck

There are lots of curious customs connected with New Year's Eve and New Year's Day. Here's what people do around the world to guarantee themselves good luck for the next twelve months.

Eat round fruits. In Spain and Italy it's grapes. Exactly twelve of them. Each one will bring a month of good fortune. In the Philippines it's any kind of fruit as long as it's the right shape.

Bang on pots. This is in New Zealand. The louder you bang on the frying pans and saucepans the better, because the noise scares away evil spirits. The Japanese do the same thing: at midnight they ring the church bells 108 times to drive out the old year and release people from their temptations (because according to the Buddhist religion, as many as 108 temptations prevent us from achieving perfect happiness).

Put on clothes of a particular color. In Brazil you have to dress in white because in that country white symbolizes purity—dressed in white, we enter the new year pure and free of all our past burdens. In other South American countries the color of the clothes you wear on New Year's Eve also has significance: red underclothes herald love in the year ahead, yellow ones mean wealth, and blue ones good health.

Light a bonfire. The Scottish New Year's celebration, known as Hogmanay, starts with a great parade. The people taking part in the procession carry flaming firebrands, and then at the city center they set fire to a Viking longboat (the Vikings were the sworn enemies who once invaded the Scottish lands). On the dot of midnight, the sky is ablaze with fireworks. The fun goes on until January 2, and it's accompanied by numerous concerts. On New Year's Eve and New Year's Day the Scots love to visit one another's homes. They make sure the first person to cross the threshold is a tall, dark-haired man, because for centuries those with fair or red hair have been associated with the cruel Vikings.

Party in the street. Since 1904, New Yorkers have traditionally gathered at midnight in Times Square, the busiest junction in the city, where the huge, shining Times Square ball is set up on top of one of the skyscrapers. When the clock strikes twelve, the glittering ball drops several dozen feet, and multicolored confetti showers down on the cheering crowds.

Enter the New Year together. Or jump into it. Literally! In Argentina, just before midnight strikes, the people partying stop dancing, pick up their champagne glasses, and stand on their left foot. As the clock strikes twelve, everyone puts his or her left foot down at the same moment. Meanwhile, in Denmark people stand on chairs, and then everyone jumps off them at the same moment.

Break crockery. This is done by the Danes. They're supposed to gain good luck in the new year by smashing old plates, glasses, and bowls outside their friends' doors. They do it on the morning of January 1. The Greeks smash something too, but it's pomegranates.

Paint dolls. The morning of January 1 is special for the Japanese too. On that day families gather before their household altars and make their wishes for the year ahead. They hold daruma dolls made of papier-mâché or wood, which look a bit like Russian Matryoshka dolls or roly-poly toys. They have no arms or legs, but they have huge heads with empty spaces for painting in the eyes. The person making the wish paints the doll's left eye and then puts

it on a shelf. Some time later when the wish comes true, the owner of the doll paints in the second eye and so restores its full vision, which is a way of saying thank-you for its help. If the wish is not fulfilled, the daruma is burned at the temple as a punishment on the next New Year's Day. At the same time, the doll that has made the wish come true is supposed to be burned too, otherwise it'll bring bad luck.

Wait for a blessing. Before noon on New Year's Day the residents of Rome and a vast number of tourists gather in Saint Peter's Square to see the pope, because January 1 is celebrated as the World Day of Peace, established in 1967 by Pope Paul VI. The pope emerges onto a balcony of Saint Peter's cathedral and delivers an address calling for an end to wars and for good deeds to be done. Then at midnight he gives the people his best wishes for the new year and ceremonially blesses them. He does it in memory of the night from the year 999 to 1000 when Silvester II, overjoyed that the predicted end of the world had not occurred, appeared a window of his palace and wished everybody good fortune.

The adoration of the kings

The Bible only mentions them in one place: guided by a star, they came to Bethlehem to bow to Jesus and offer him gold, frankincense, and myrrh. So who were the three kings?

In fact, nobody knows if they really did exist. The Bible doesn't mention their names, though in popular culture they are called Caspar, Melchior, and Baltazar, or even their number—the idea that there were three of them was assumed from the number of gifts they brought. They're known as the three kings, the three wise men, or the three magi. For centuries they've been presented as rulers from the East, traveling in a rich procession, wise astrologers, or plain wanderers. They came to Bethlehem because, according to a prophecy known to them, a child had been born there who in the future would be the mightiest ruler in the world. We celebrate the feast of the three kings on January 6. On that day the carnival begins. In some countries, including Spain, the three kings bring the children presents.

The Three Kings is the customary name of this holiday, in popular terms. In fact, on January 6 we're really celebrating the Feast of the Epiphany. Epiphany (meaning "revelation") has to do with three events that "revealed God to the world"—in other words, they provided proof that Jesus is God. They were: the adoration of the three kings, the baptism of the adult Jesus in the Jordan River, and the miracle Jesus performed when he changed water into wine at the wedding at Cana. But Epiphany is usually only associated with the first of these events, hence its common name. To mark the occasion, processions of the three kings are organized in cities around the world. The Portuguese and the French also bake crown-shaped "king cakes": the Portuguese ones (called bolos de reis) have a dried bean inside, and French ones (galettes des rois) include an almond. The lucky person who finds the bean or the almond is given a paper crown and becomes king.

On the Feast of the Epiphany the Poles draw the letters *C+M+B* on the doors of their homes and add the number of the new year. It is commonly believed that *C*, *M*, and *B* are the first letters of the names of the three kings. But in fact these initials stand for the Latin words *Christus mansionem benedicat*: "May Christ bless this house." Some people also interpret the initials as the first letters of words that describe the three events of Epiphany: *cogito*— "I recognize" (because the three kings recognized Jesus), *baptesimus*—baptism, and *matrimonium*—a wedding.

Delicious coal

There's one country where, on January 6, as well as the three kings, someone else appears too. Someone ugly, in shoes full of holes and a patched dress but with a good heart. That country is Italy, and the visitor is Befana.

She flies to the children on a broomstick, and she's an old, poorly dressed woman. She squeezes her way down the chimney and puts presents in their socks. But watch out—she's not as understanding as Santa Claus! She leaves

lumps of coal for the naughty children, though later they often turn out to be candies that just look unappetizing.

According to legend, when the three kings were on their way to the stable to see the newborn baby Jesus, they met an old woman. They told her where they were going and invited her to come along with them, but she refused, pleading pressing obligations. Once the three kings had vanished over the horizon, she regretted her decision and tried to catch up with them, but they were already too far away. Ever since, the old woman has roamed the world. According to one version, she peeps into all the houses where there are children in the hope of seeing the baby Jesus, and while she's there she leaves small gifts; and according to another version, she delivers the presents she failed to give to Jesus to all the other children.

In Italy they say: *L'Epifania tutte le feste le porta via*, which means literally "Epiphany takes all the other holidays with it." Befana heralds the inevitable end of the festive season.

In Venice, on the feast of the three kings, Befana regattas are held—oarsmen dressed up as witches race their boats along the Grand Canal, the biggest canal in the city. The participants are members of the oldest rowing club in Venice, the Bucintoro, and the race lasts for around fifteen minutes. The finish line is at the city's biggest bridge, the Rialto, and on this day there's an enormous sock hanging from it. After the race the oarsmen, residents, and tourists enjoy refreshments including mulled wine and snacks served at stalls set up for the occasion.

In the town of Urbania, Befana spectacularly flies down to the marketplace from the bell tower roof and then sits in a wooden cottage specially prepared

for her, where she greets the children, tells them fairy tales, and reveals her secrets. Right next door there's a post office where the youngest children can leave letters listing the presents they'd like to receive a year from now. Finally, the local people walk in procession down the main street of the town, the Corso Vittorio Emanuele II, carrying a stocking that's dozens of yards long. Hundreds of socks, both large and small, flutter in all the windows, and dancing and performances of various kinds continue late into the night.

A delayed holiday

In some countries the religious festivals are celebrated according to the so-called Julian calendar. That's why in Russia, Ethiopia, and Ukraine Christmas doesn't take place until January.

In Russia, Ukraine, and Belarus the main religion is Orthodox Christianity. The people are Christians, like many Europeans and Americans, but their customs and liturgy (the way they pray) are slightly different. Christmas is an obvious example of this. Above all, it starts on January 7 (January 6 is Christmas Eve), and it lasts for not two but three days. On the first day the birth of Christ is celebrated at the Orthodox churches, on the second the Virgin Mary is worshipped, and on the third it's Saint Stephen, the first martyr, who gave

his life for his faith. Apart from that, everything else is similar to the other Christian festivals: similar dishes appear on the table (including carp, cabbage, and beet soup as in Poland), and the houses and churches are decorated with Christmas trees. Only the Christmas cribs are missing, but instead there are icons (religious paintings) showing the stable in Bethlehem and the Holy Family sheltering inside it.

The Christmas period doesn't end until January 19, on the Feast of Jordan, which commemorates the day when the adult Jesus was baptized. After the service, the priests and the congregation walk in a ceremonial procession to the banks of the nearest river, pond, or lake and consecrate the water by dipping a cross in it three times. If the water is frozen, they cut a hole in the ice in the shape of a cross. The congregation scoop the consecrated water into bottles and take it home because they believe it has healing powers.

The Christians in Ethiopia celebrate the holiday in a completely different way. Here there are no Christmas trees or stable, but there's a lot of singing and dancing. Christmas, known to the Ethiopians as Genna or Lidet, starts on the evening of January 6. Dressed in white and led by a priest dressed in golden robes, the believers walk in a ceremonial procession from church to church. They sing as they go and dance to the beat of music played on drums, rattles, lyres, and pipes. Next day they meet again in church, this time for a Christmas Mass that's held at 4:00 a.m.

As the Ethiopian masses and processions go on for a long time, the congregation lean on distinctive prayer staffs shaped like the letter *T*, and the priest has a similar one too. In addition, a brightly colored parasol is carried above the priest to protect him from the sun.

During Lidet a traditional chicken appears on the Ethiopian table, in a spicy sauce known as doro wat. After finishing their meal, the children are given gifts, usually new clothes, and the young people play genna, which is a kind of field hockey (and which is named for the holiday).

On the holiday of Timkat, which takes place thirteen days later (it was established on January 19 to commemorate the baptism of Christ), processions appear in the streets again. This time the congregation carry copies of the Ark of the Covenant in their parades. The ark is the name of the box in which the two stone tablets inscribed with the ten commandments were found. These were the laws people were to obey in order to live in consensus and harmony. For centuries the Ark was kept in Solomon's Temple in Jerusalem, but when the temple was destroyed, the Ark disappeared. The Ethiopians believe it is hidden in their country. Every Ethiopian church keeps a copy of the ark that's displayed at Timkat.

Glossary

Merry Christmas!

Feliz Navidad!—in Spanish [felis navidad]

Frohe Weihnachten!—in German [fro-er vynakhten]

Joyeux Noël!—in French [jwy-a no-wel]

Buon Natale!—in Italian [buon natale]

Wesołych Świąt!—in Polish [vessa-weekh shvee-yont]

Santa Claus

Father Christmas—in Great Britain

Ded Moroz (Grandpa Frost)—in Russian [dyed maroz]

Père Noël—in French [pair no-wel]

Babbo Natale—in Italian [babbo natale]

Weihnachtsmann (Christmas Visitor)—in northern and western regions of Germany [vynakhtsman]

Mikołaj—in Poland [meeko-why]

Sinterklaas—the Dutch name for Saint Nicholas, who visits the children on December 5 and is dressed in traditional bishop's robes [sinterklas]

Kerstman—the Dutch name for Saint Nicholas when he visits children on December 25 and looks like the American Santa Claus [kerstman]

Julemanden—in Danish [yu-lemanden]

Viejito Pascuero (the Old Shepherd)—in Chilean Spanish [vee-ehito pasku-ero]

First published in the United States, Great Britain, Canada, Australia, and New Zealand in 2021 by NorthSouth Books Inc., an imprint of NordSüd Verlag AG, CH-8050 Zürich, Switzerland.
Distributed in the United States by NorthSouth Books Inc., New York 10016.
Library of Congress Cataloging-in-Publication Data is available.
ISBN: 978-0-7358-4443-8
Printed by Livonia Print, Riga, Latvia

FSC
www.fsc.org
MIX
Paper from
responsible sources
FSC® C002795